Photo Credits

Ryu Seunghoo, Cover, 4, 5, 6, 8, 10, 15, 18, 23, 24, 29, 30, 31, 32, 38, 40, 41, 42-47, 49-51, 53-55, 74, 80-81, 85, 92, 108, 112, 114, 124-125

Image Korea, 34, 96, 100-101

Hong Kyeong-hee, 16, 37, 56

Robert J. Koehler, 20, 36

Marc Matsumoto, 102, 106

Jung hee-won, 66, 69

Jang Seo-hee, 88

Xinhua News Agency, 76

Paintings in the Chapter "Some Korean Tea Poems" courtesy of the artist **Gu Ji-hoe**

Sixth printing in 2021

First published in 2007 by Seoul Selection
105-2 Sagan-dong, Jongno-gu, Seoul, Korea
Phone (82-2) 734-9567, Fax (82-2) 734-9562
Email: publisher@seoulselection.com

Published in the Republic of Korea
by Seoul Selection
ISBN: 978-89-91913-17-2

Printed in the Republic of Korea
http://www.seoulselection.com

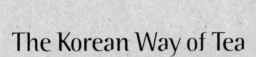

The Korean Way of Tea

An Introductory Guide

Brother Anthony of Taizé and Hong Kyeong-Hee

Contents

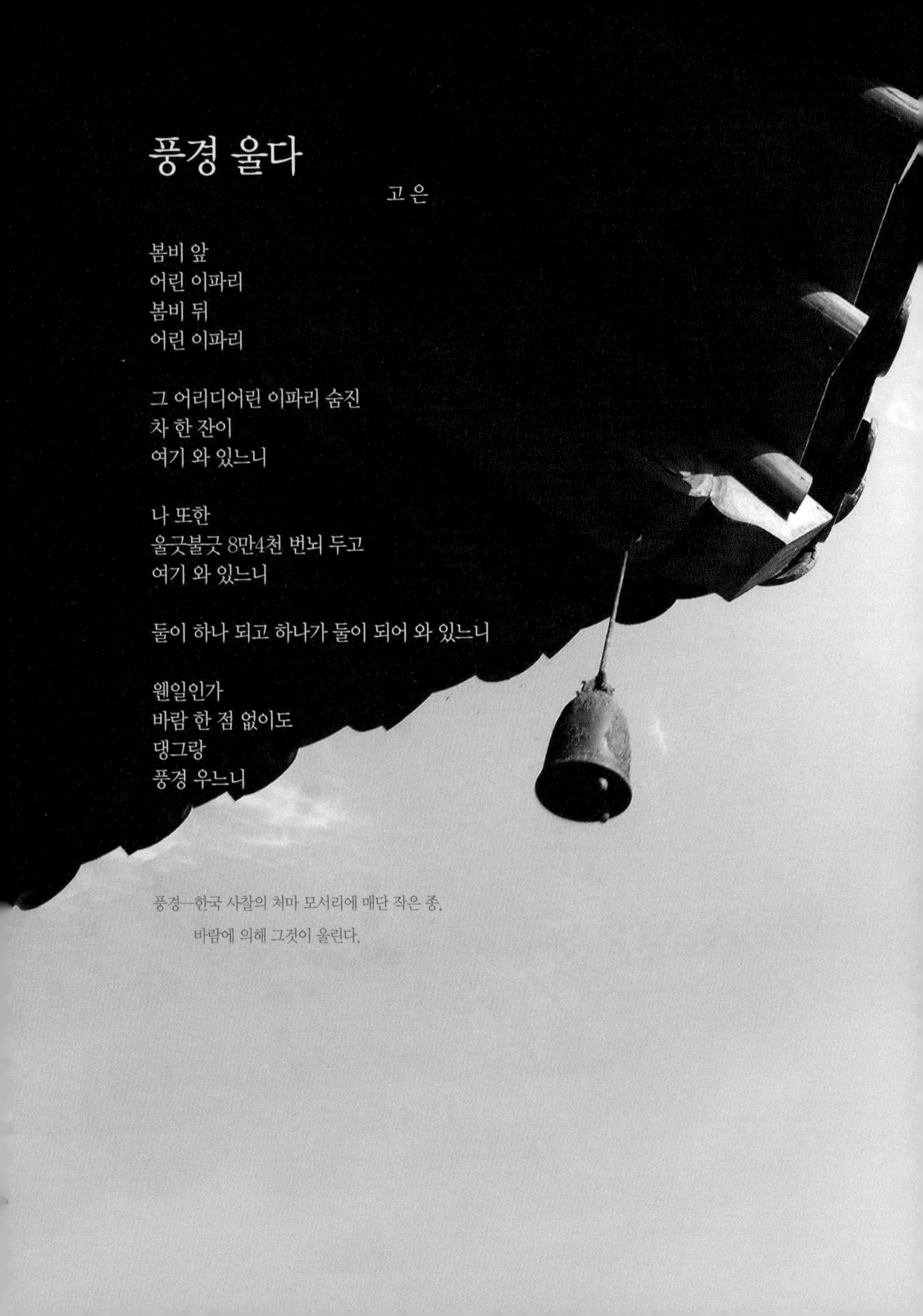

풍경 울다

고 은

봄비 앞
어린 이파리
봄비 뒤
어린 이파리

그 어리디어린 이파리 숨진
차 한 잔이
여기 와 있느니

나 또한
울긋불긋 8만4천 번뇌 두고
여기 와 있느니

둘이 하나 되고 하나가 둘이 되어 와 있느니

웬일인가
바람 한 점 없이도
댕그랑
풍경 우느니

풍경—한국 사찰의 처마 모서리에 매단 작은 종.
　　　바람에 의해 그것이 울린다.

A *wind-bell is ringing*

by Ko Un

Before spring rain—
a baby leaf.
After spring rain—
a baby leaf.

That tiny little baby leaf has died
so one cup of tea
has arrived here

I too
leaving behind eighty-four thousand bright-hued passions
have arrived here.

Two becoming one, one becoming two, we are here.

What's this?
There's not a breath of wind yet
—ting-a-ling—
a wind-bell is ringing!

Note: A wind-bell is a small bell hanging from the eaves of a temple,
that rings when the wind catches a vane (often fish-shaped) attached to its clapper.

The Mystery in a Cup of Tea

If you have never tasted Korean green tea, you might be wondering what, if anything, could justify writing a whole book about it. The best way of explaining would be to go together to the southern slopes of Jiri Mountain, way down south from Seoul, in late April or early May. Sitting in a traditional Korean house, with doors and windows open to the early morning sunshine, well away from any road with its lingering exhaust fumes, we would watch as our hostess prepares tea she herself dried only a day or two before, using very small, just-budded leaves. The water for brewing the tea is drawn from a stone basin fed by a spring that rises just behind the house. We can hear a mountain stream gushing over boulders down the valley in front of us, and all the trees around are in their freshest green. The taste of the first cup of tea, made with water that is far below boiling point, on a palate freshly awakened, is so intense, so unexpectedly rich and varied, so indescribably fragrant, that from that day on the only question can be: "When shall I be able to go back and drink that tea again?"

Even in Korea, the finest green tea is not easily obtained. As in many parts of today's world, it is easy to buy boxes of one-cup tea bags of green tea at very low cost, but as soon as it comes to leaf tea, the difference in price is considerable. The small quantities of high-quality tea made by hand on the slopes of Korea's southern mountains are sometimes sold for very high prices, especially early in the season.

Then again, the names by which good Korean tea is sold are also confusing, even for Koreans. Virtually all the Korean tea produced is green tea. But on the box or pack, very often the tea is called *Jakseol-cha* (sparrow's tongue tea), a traditional term stressing the small size of the leaves, but with no other particular meaning. *Nok-cha* (green tea) is a term that seems mostly to be associated with tea-bags, and it is not often used on boxes of better-quality tea; in fact, it is a recently-invented name, created to distinguish "green tea" from Western-style "red tea." Another traditional name given to green tea is *Jungno-cha* (bamboo dew tea).

Usually, the name given to the tea is a poetic one, whether it be *Panyaro* (Dew of Wisdom), *Gwan-hyang* (Fragrant view), *Dongsan-cha* (East-Mountain tea), or *Ok-no* (Jade dew). These names tell you nothing about the tea in the box. If the tea grows more or less freely, naturally, with minimal fertilizing and trimming, it is known as *Yasaeng-cha* (wild tea). This is in contrast to the tea that grows in long, tidy rows in large-scale plantations; Koreans always feel that what grows naturally will be better than what is cultivated artificially. In the end, the main difference is between hand-dried and machine-dried teas, tea made on a small scale by individuals and tea produced by machines in a factory. Nothing on the boxes indicates the mode of production.

The most common way of indicating different grades of quality involves using the labels *Ujeon* (tea made in April), *Sejak* (tea made in later April – early May) and *Jungjak* (tea made in May). These correspond more or less to the "first flush, second flush, third flush" of high quality Indian teas. *Ujeon*, made of the smallest, earliest shoots, is always the most expensive, and sometimes quite excessively so. *Sejak* is usually almost as good, at least, despite using shoots that emerged slightly later. A good producer's *Jungjak* will be only a little less intensely flavored, having been made later in May than the other two. It will usually be quite a bit cheaper. Buyers need to know that sometimes *Ujeon* can lose part of its special fragrance after only a few months, even if sealed in a foil packet; it is not necessarily the best buy by the time Christmas comes.

Perhaps all of that helps to explain why, in Korea, there are relatively few people who regularly drink good green tea. It is in part a matter of quantities, and of price. Anyone traveling through the southern regions of Japan is accustomed to seeing serried green ranks of tea bushes almost everywhere. There, a cup of simply brewed green tea is automatically offered wherever one goes. If we cross the sea to the regions of China west and south of Shanghai, or to Taiwan, large tea plantations can easily be found. Tea, in various forms drunk in various ways, is the staple form of refreshment everywhere in China. Going with Korean friends into a "traditional tea-room," you will often discover that they do not even know how to serve Korean green tea using a teapot and cups!

In Korea, extensive areas planted in tea are very few and far between. The climate is not favorable, it seems, but above all until recently there has been virtually no market for green tea; coffee or other beverages are usually preferred. Even when green tea in a tea-bag is available, it often proves to have been combined with powdered whole-grain rice to yield a rounder, sweeter taste; moreover, there is always a suspicion that the tea in the bag may have been imported from some neighboring country where it is so much cheaper. In Seoul, green tea from a small number of recognized producers, individual and industrial, can be bought in the up-market department stores. Other, often better teas, have to be looked for in specialized shops and tea-rooms, or obtained directly from the producer.

So this book will not be of much direct help to people shopping for green tea in San Francisco or London. They will have to search hard to find any kind of Korean green tea, while Japanese and Chinese varieties are relatively common. Korean tea, especially the very finest, is rare, hard to find, and quite expensive. Nonetheless,

The view from a countryside *chabang* in Hadong, South Gyeongsang Province

Tea plantation in Boseong, South Jeolla Province

it is at last becoming possible to find good Korean tea in Europe and North America at prices that are comparable with those for really good Chinese or Japanese teas. So this book has been written in the hope that in the years to come more will be produced, more will be exported, and more tea-lovers will come to Korea in search of teas unlike those produced anywhere else.

Korean green tea is essentially Korean. At its very best it has almost nothing in common with Japanese or Chinese tea, beyond the mystery that all are made using leaves from the same plant.

Newcomers to tea never fail to be amazed on learning that all the tea drunk in the world, no matter whether it is white, green, yellow, oolong, red, brown, or black, and no matter where it comes from, is made of the leaves of the same evergreen tree or bush. The story of how the different kinds of tea were developed is quite a poetic one. We shall try to tell it later in this book.

Green tea is tea in its purest, most immediate form. The newly budded leaves are dried quickly, freshly picked from the tree at the time when they have their most intense taste. Many other kinds of teas have been developed, their characteristic flavors depending on a slower drying process. This allows the fresh leaf to wilt, the juices within it to oxidize. This produces the immense variety of tastes in the Chinese teas known collectively as "Oolong" (Black Dragon). As the green color fades, the leaves grow increasingly reddish brown, and the fully oxidized tea leaves, called "red tea" by the Chinese, are in the West known as "black" tea. Most of the tea drunk in the world is of this latter kind, but in recent years people in many countries have begun to realize the special virtues of green tea. Usually, they look to China (where "Dragon Well" is the most familiar name), to Japan, or to Darjeeling for their health-giving green teas. We want to invite readers of these pages to look to Korea instead.

Tea in Korea

Where does tea grow?

Tea bushes were probably first brought to Korea some fifteen hundred years ago, from China. But the custom of drinking tea gradually weakened and for much of the 20th century, tea was hardly cultivated in Korea. In the hilly southern regions, the only part of the country where the tea tree will grow, bushes continued to grow in the wild. Because it cannot survive harsh winter frosts, tea does not grow north of Jeonju (North Jeolla Province) and it cannot thrive on every kind of soil even to the south. The tea bush prefers an acid soil rich in organic matter. Country folk always recognized the medicinal qualities of the leaves, boiling them to produce an intensely bitter but seemingly effective cure for winter colds and fevers.

The first attempt to cultivate tea in modern times began in the southwestern province of South Jeolla, in Boseong. There, tea

Tea plantation in Hadong, South Gyeongsang Province

cultivation started in 1939, during the Japanese colonial period. Japanese tea specialists selected the area as an ideal place for black tea cultivation and started planting imported Indian tea seeds. After Independence in 1945, the tea plantation there was abandoned. It was taken up again in the late 1950s. Today, Boseong's tea plantations have become a major tourist attraction with more than 1.5 million visitors annually, many attracted by seeing the tea fields used as the setting for romantic television dramas. Another plantation originally started by the Japanese is one located on the slopes of Mudeung-san Mountain in Gwangju (South Jeolla Province), where the artist Uijei Heo Baek-nyeon produced tea for many years until his death in 1977.

Historically, however, the southern slopes of Jiri Mountain have long been associated with the finest tea. There, the presence of a number of Buddhist temples helped to stimulate an interest in using the wild tea that grew plentifully in some areas. The wild tea trees growing on the slopes of hills in Hadong county, between the temples of Ssanggye-sa and Dasol-sa, especially provided supplies of delicately-flavored leaves in springtime. It is probably no coincidence that the modern tea revival began with the Venerable Hyodang, who was for many years the head monk of Dasol-sa Temple, which lies between Hadong and Jinju.

Monks in temples of the area were accustomed to pick and dry the fresh tea leaves in springtime for drinking, and slowly production grew as more Koreans became aware of their tea tradition. In recent years more and more tea has been planted on the slopes of Jiri-san between Hadong and Hwagye, and other southern hills, too, but without the creation of large, industrialized tea plantations of the kind that characterize Boseong or Jeju Island. The finest tea is that grown in complete harmony with nature and with only very limited use of fertilizers; the best growers refuse to use any kind of insecticides that could contaminate the leaves.

When is Korean green tea made?

Good green tea can only be made using the fresh tips, the scarcely opened buds that start to grow in middle or late April. Once a leaf is fully developed, it is soon too coarse for use. After late May the bushes may continue to produce further shoots but these no longer have the intense flavor needed for good tea. Therefore all the green tea needed for the year has to be plucked and dried in a little over one month. The very earliest buds have the finest flavor, and are the most difficult to collect. If the winter frosts last late, the buds may only begin to sprout in later April. Rain, too, is needed if the bushes are to produce a second and third growth of buds rapidly to replace those that have been picked, but picking has to stop during rainy spells, since it is not possible to make tea if the leaves are wet.

The traditional Korean calendar was lunar, but still today it has twenty-four seasonal dates based on the movement of the sun, which it borrowed, together with their names, from Chinese tradition. The day known as *Gok-u* normally falls on April 20. The tea picked before this date, the first budding, is known as *Ujeon* and commands the highest price. The next seasonal date *Ipha* falls on May 5 or 6, and tea gathered between those two dates, mostly the second budding, is known as *Sejak*. Tea gathered after *Ipha* is known as *Jungjak*. These names (also of Chinese origin) often figure on the menus in tea-rooms, to the mystification of the uninformed public. It should be added that the Korean weather is colder than that in southern China, with the result that

An inviting path to Gwanhyang Dawon

Korean tea-makers, although they pay lip-service to the traditional dates, actually go on making *Ujeon* from the first growth of shoots even after April 20, when very often there are still virtually no fresh shoots on the tea bushes. *Sejak*, too, may continue to be made so long as the leaves are sufficiently small and intensely flavored.

Picking the tea

The gathering of the fresh tea buds requires skill and speed. Mostly the women of the region do it, but even the most quick-handed can only collect a few pounds of leaves in the course of a day. The bud in question is composed ideally of one freshly opened leaf, the half-unrolled leaf above it, and the bud of a third leaf still needle-like at the tip of the stalk. Traditionally, Korean green tea is often called "*Jakseol-cha*" (sparrows' tongues tea) since it is made of only the smallest leaves, barely more than buds, unlike many Chinese teas. In some of the very largest tea fields, those found in Jeju Island, for example, tea is sometimes gathered by machine

but that means that a lot of older leaves, as well as stems and twigs, get mixed with the shoots. Even with careful sorting, that is obviously going to affect the quality of the tea produced. With handpicked tea, too, care is needed and the first task after the leaves arrive at the drying area is to spread them on a clean rush mat and carefully remove any twigs, old and damaged leaves, and weeds that have got mixed among them.

The 19th-century monk Cho Ui composed a guide to the Way of Tea, *Tasin-jeon*, in which he wrote:

Regarding the season of picking tea leaves, the right time is important. If it is too early, the fragrance of the tea will not be complete; if it is too late, the spirit of the tea will be scattered. Purple tea buds are the best and wrinkled leaves are the second; round leaves are the next, while leaves that shine bright and look like dwarf bamboo are worst. It is best to pick leaves that have been soaked with dew during a cloudless night; picking leaves in sunshine comes the next; picking leaves when it is cloudy or raining is not appropriate. Tea leaves produced in a valley are the best; leaves growing under a bamboo forest are the second; leaves grown in stony ground are third; and leaves that grow in yellow sand are the next.

Making Tea

The drying of the leaves to produce green tea must be done rapidly, and be completed before the juices in them start to oxidize. That means that leaves picked in the course of one day have to be dried during the following day. After the leaves are delivered to the place where they are to be dried, they are often left to spend the night uncovered in the open air, piled loosely. There is a belief that the final taste will be better if the leaves absorb the moonlight and starlight, and also the dew, providing it is not heavy enough to make them really damp.

In Korea as in Japan, the easiest, industrial method of drying green tea involves the use of a revolving drum in which the leaves are dried by hot air as the drum turns. This is the method used in the large-scale production of green tea in Boseong and Jeju Island, and almost everywhere in Japan. But the result is that the leaves get broken by the rough treatment they undergo in the machines; moreover, since machines cannot take account of small variations in the size or quality of the leaves, the taste is never equal to that found in tea that has been dried by hand in small quantities in the traditional manner.

Nothing is more challenging than to make tea by hand. Much of the finest tea is made by devoted laypersons and Buddhist monks, who regard the task as a spiritual discipline requiring great concentration. Certainly, no one can expect to earn money or fame by tea-making; it can only be done as a labor of love, as a service to those who practice the Way of Tea. Some people begin each day's tea-making with prayers, meditation and reading of scriptures. Ideally, perhaps, the person making the tea should also pick the leaves but this is not usually possible. The leaves must come from bushes that are located well away from any road, for tea readily absorbs the smell of exhaust fumes. Likewise, those making tea must not use any perfumed soap or cosmetics for the same reason. Externally and inwardly, there must be real cleanliness, simplicity of mind, and devotion of heart.

The leaves, too, have to be carefully selected, especially when making the finest tea by hand. It is a little like wine-making, for certain patches of ground yield leaves that are particularly fragrant while other parts of the same valley or hill are incapable of producing tea of that quality. Some plantation-owners apply liberal doses of fertilizer, which encourages the rapid growth of insipid leaves; obviously, there must be no trace of insecticide on the fresh buds used for making tea, but in some plantations even that is not guaranteed! People making tea need to check very carefully where the leaves they use have been picked, if they do not pick their own.

There are two main methods of hand-drying in use in Korea when making the best green tea, *Bucheo-cha* and *Jeung-cha*. The way of drying resulting in what is known as *Bucheo-cha* is the most common. About three kilograms of fresh leaves are dried at a time.

Parching

The drying is done in a thick iron or steel cauldron, which is traditionally heated by a wood fire although nowadays a gas ring is often used, since that allows easier control of the temperature. The cauldron is first heated to about 350 degrees Celsius then the fresh leaves are tipped in.

The leaves may emit a hissing crackle as they touch the hot metal. They must be tossed gently and stirred constantly to prevent any burning. This softens them; then once they have absorbed the heat, they are briefly compressed and rolled together to encourage the evaporation of their moisture. Often two people work together to keep the leaves turning, hunched over the hot cauldron in what is a truly back-breaking task.

Rolling

After an initial time of softening and drying over the fire, the leaves are removed from the heat and rubbed and rolled vigorously by the palms of the hands on a firm flat surface, often a rough straw mat or basket, so that they curl tightly on themselves. This encourages the development of an intense taste but if too much violence is used the leaves will tear and break and the quality of the tea will suffer. Speed and strength are both essential here.

Counter-clockwise from left:
- The leaves are flattened out to dry
- Dried tea leaves are placed over a wood fire for another round of parching
- Jirisan tea is best parched over a wood fire like the one pictured here

Separating

The next step is the most delicate and time-consuming. The emerging juices make the rolled leaves tend to stick tightly together, and they have to be shaken apart one by one in order that their moisture can evaporate freely. Without this, the tea cannot dry properly, but if too much force is used, the leaves will tear and break.

Throughout the entire drying process, older leaves, twigs and harder stalks must continue to be removed. The partially dried leaves may next be spread thinly on paper laid on trays and left exposed to the air while other batches of fresh leaves are dried.

By the end of the first cycle of drying and rolling, the leaves have already diminished considerably in

volume. They are now put back in the cauldron, which is rather cooler than for the first drying though still quite hot. Again they are turned, pressed, rolled gently as the drying continues. Then the hot leaves are once again removed from the cauldron, rubbed and rolled together on a hard surface, and shaken apart.

Once again they are given a short time to go on drying in the air. Then the same process is repeated, several times, until they are virtually dry. Traditionally, tea was supposed to be dried and rolled nine times (*gujeung-gupo*) but today tea-makers usually reckon that three or four times are enough.

The emerging juices make the rolled leaves tend to stick tightly together, and they have to be shaken apart one by one in order that their moisture can evaporate freely

Throughout the entire drying process, older leaves, twigs and harder stalks must continue to be removed

Final Drying

The nearly-dry leaves are spread out thinly and allowed to go on drying on sheets of clean paper spread on the heated floor of an indoors room for at least 4-5 hours, often overnight.

They are then returned to the cauldron that is now only lightly heated, and kept turning gently, all the time being stirred and pressed, until the leaves are completely dry. This is the decisive final process, known in Korean as *mat-naegi* or *hyang-olligi* (taste-giving or fragrance-enhancing), lasting several hours. As the drying progresses, the leaves emit a pale cloud of intense fragrance. By the end of it all, their color has changed from the bright green of the picked leaves to a dark gray hue. Yet when they are brewed, they revert to their original fresh green color.

Once the tea is completely dry, it is given time to cool before being packed. This is important, since tea that is too quickly sealed may retain a taste of roasting that will spoil it. Korean tea is not usually vacuum packed, but is sealed in foil bags containing 50 grams in the case of *ujeon* and 50 or 100 grams for other grades. The most important thing is to prevent any contact with moisture. The tea should be stored in a cool place and once a pack is opened, it should be used up fairly quickly,

especially in the case of *ujeon*, which can easily lose its delicate taste once exposed to the air.

Jeung-cha

The other method of tea-making yields the tea known as **Jeung-cha**. Here, the fresh leaves are plunged for a moment into nearly boiling water, then allowed to drain on mats for a couple of hours, before being placed in a cauldron over a wood fire. The initial dipping into hot water that characterizes *Jeung-cha* is much more commonly found in Japanese methods of tea-making than in Korea, but after the initial stage there is little similarity in the way of making this tea in the two countries. The resulting Korean tea is completely different in color, taste and fragrance.

With *Jeung-cha*, the drying and rolling are done concurrently, the leaves are not removed from the heat until they are dry, after two or three hours. During this time, the leaves are constantly turned, rubbed, rolled and pressed to the bottom of the cauldron. The drying has to be completely regular and at the same time no leaf must burn. Not surprisingly, this tea, which has by far the finest fragrance, is very rare. The best known is that produced by Chae Won-Hwa, in accordance with the method she learned from the Venerable Hyodang.

Experience

The most important factor in making fine tea by hand is experience. Every year the weather in winter and up into April is different, warmer or colder, wetter or dryer. That has a big influence on the date and the quality of the first buds of the tea bushes. Likewise, the weather while the tea is being made has to be considered, whether it is a still or windy day, whether the air is humid or dry. The size and quality of the leaves varies, too. At every stage, there are many variables that influence the final result: knowing when and by how much to increase or diminish the heat being used, when to remove a batch of leaves from the fire,

whether a batch needs further drying or not.,

  In those parts of Jiri Mountain where the best tea is produced; you will usually find that one or two elderly women have been doing a lot of the hardest work drying the tea ever since serious tea-making began in the 1970s under the direction of monks and masters. Intuition, not science, is the key to tea; these women have no thermometers or stopwatches to guide them. They just know what needs to be done, at every moment, and without them even the greatest tea master is helpless. One of the major uncertainties about the future of Korean tea is whether their practice will continue in subsequent generations. Not many younger people in today's Korea are ready to work so hard for so little money, even in the countryside.

From Cho Ui's *Tasin-jeon*

It is hard to describe in words, but experience, skill, and intuition are needed to manufacture tea. If heating was appropriate in terms of balance and process, the color and scent of the tea become beautiful. After such delicate efforts, both the spirit and taste of the tea will be subtle and wonderful. The excellence of tea exists at first in the care of manufacturing, then in the management of proper storage, and right or appropriate infusion of boiled water. Superior and inferior tea are first determined in the roasting pan; purity and impurity of the tea are related to fire and water. If the fire is strong, the scent of tea will be clean; if overheated, the spirit of tea decreases. When the fire is fierce, the tea leaves are burnt; when firewood is insufficient, the leaves lose their blue color; when firing is too long, the leaves become overdone.

Top: 19th-century Buddhist monk Cho Ui (1786-1866)
Bottom: Ilchi-am, the hermitage residence of Cho Ui

It should be noted that in recent years, Korean tea-makers have also begun producing small quantities of oxidized tea, usually known as *Hwang-cha* (yellow tea), that is similar in taste to the black/red tea familiar to the rest of the world. This kind of tea was traditionally produced in the Hwagye district, under the name of *Jaeksal-cha*.

Brewing Green Tea

T he water used for preparing the most delicately flavored kinds of Korean green tea should be well below boiling point, and for the first cup of a really good tea, water as low as 50 degrees may sometimes produce the best results. If the water is too hot, or is allowed to remain too long on the leaves, the finest taste is lost and the bitter elements emerge. For many kinds of green tea, however, almost boiling water can be used as it is for all kinds of oxidized tea.

The water used for making tea should be pure spring water. The Chinese have developed a great sensitivity about this, and the most famous teas are each supposed to be drunk using only water from this or that particular well. Chlorinated tap water can ruin the taste of any tea!

Traditionally the water should be boiled in a kettle on a charcoal fire in a small brasero in the tea-room; there are many poems about the various levels of sound as the water sings on the

Tea set arranged on a low wooden table

fire, slowly reaching the point where it sounds like wind rustling in bamboos or pines. Today most people use electric pots, which are less poetic but much simpler. A brasero is still used when preparing tea to be offered at ancestral memorial ceremonies.

In order to prepare green tea in the Korean way, a tea set (*cha-gi*) is used. These are usually designed for serving tea for three to five people. Most Korean sets are made of stoneware pottery, and tend to be quite simple and rustic in design and decoration, rather than displaying the high sophistication of English bone ware or Chinese porcelain. The standard tea set consists of the following items:

1   The tea pot (*cha-gwan* or *cha urineun jujeonja*). This is the most important item; Korean pots are much smaller than those used in the West for black tea. The opening at the top, closed by the lid, should be wide enough for the tea leaves and water to enter easily and cleanly. The

spout should be high enough not to overflow when the pot is completely full. It should pour cleanly without any drops running down to the foot of the pot. The perforations in the body of the pot to filter out the leaves must be large enough for the tea to flow freely on pouring but small enough to retain quite small fragments of leaf. Usually the handle is shaped as a cylinder projecting from the side of the pot at 90 degrees to the spout; it should be large enough

The tea pot
(*cha-gwan* or *cha urineun jujeonja*)

to be grasped firmly; some pots have looped handles opposite the spout, or a hoop in bamboo or pottery rising above the pot. It is usually good to have several pots, and to use the one best suited to the number of people being served. If several different kinds of tea with strongly contrasting tastes are regularly made, each kind of tea should be made using a different tea pot, although the contrasts in Korean tea are less intense than with Chinese teas.

2   The cups (*chat-jan* or *chat-jong*). These are far smaller than anything known in the West, though Chinese tea cups are often smaller still.

They have no handles, since green tea is usually made with water that is well below boiling point. Potters offer a wide variety of forms, some more open toward the top, some with quite straight sides. The cup ought to fit the hand comfortably, and permit the fragrance of the tea to emerge. The glaze should be pale enough to allow the color of the tea to be seen, though cups do not have to be pure white. Monks and people receiving a steady flow of visitors often do not bother with matching cups but have a considerable number of cups of different shapes and colors that they use at random.

3 A bowl for cooling the water before it is poured into the tea pot, and then for serving the second and subsequent brews of tea, with a lip or spout for pouring (*suk-u, mul sikhim sabal* or *gwittae-geureut*). This is usually part of the matching tea set, glazed like the pot and cups and of a suitable size for the tea pot, so that it does not have to be filled to the brim. It must pour cleanly without dribbling.

4 A large bowl into which the water used for warming the pot and

cups can be discarded (*toisu-geureut* or *toisu-gi*). This is not sold as part of a tea set, it can be any slightly larger bowl of good appearance; it lies on the floor beside the table on which the tea set is arranged.

5　A stack of saucers (*jantak* or *chat-jan batchim*). These can be made of pottery to match the cups, but usually wooden saucers are preferred for their lightness and because the cups do not grate on them.

6　A ceramic or laquerware tea caddy (*ehaho* or *chat-tong*). These are sold separately, and do not need to match exactly the glaze of the tea set. In Korea the tea is often taken directly from the box or packet in which it is sold, unless the setting is particularly elegant or formal.

7　A spoon or scoop for transferring the tea to the pot (*chasi*, *chachik* or *chacheuk*). These are made of bamboo or some other kind of odorless wood, often roughly worked in rustic mode.

8　A cloth cover (*chat-po* or *chat sang-po*). When it is not being used, the

tea set is placed on a tray and covered with a decorative cloth, traditionally red on the outside, black on the inside. Today, lighter colors are usually preferred.

9   A small folded cloth (*cha geon*) is used to wipe the vessels and mop up any drops spilled while preparing the tea.

Usually there is a small stand on which the lid of the tea pot is placed while the pot is being filled. This too is not part of the tea set. If the tea contains many broken leaves, it may be necessary to use a small strainer held just below the spout as the tea is poured. If the cups are thin and hot, a pair of bamboo pincers may be used to transfer them to the saucers.

In Korea, traditionally there were no chairs in the rooms, everyone would sit cross-legged on the floor. Today, most houses are equipped with tables and chairs, but tea is best served with everyone sitting on the floor. There are many slightly different ways of serving tea in Korea, some quite formal, some completely

relaxed. The description given here is for a fairly formal ceremony and it is not meant to be a model to be followed too rigidly.

1   The tea set is already arranged on a low wooden table (*cha-sang* or *cha-damsang*), raised only an inch or two above the floor. One person presides over the ceremony, preparing and serving the tea. That person sits behind the table, with the rest of the party in a line or half-circle on the other side.

From top left to bottom right:
- The cups, which are lying upside-down, are turned over carefully
- A first measure of hot water is poured into the lipped bowl
- The water is poured into the empty pot
- The tea is placed in the pot, using a scoop

2. The cloth covering the tea set is lifted, folded, and placed to one side.

3 The cups, which are lying upside-down, are turned over carefully, so as not to make any sound.

4 A first measure of hot water is poured into the lipped bowl. The teapot lid is removed and placed on its stand or on the folded cloth. The water is poured into the empty pot. The lid is replaced. This water warms the pot briefly.

5 It is then poured into the cups to warm them. Whenever water or tea is being poured from the teapot, the handle of the pot is held in one hand, the other hand holding the lid to prevent it from slipping off.

6 A second measure of hot water is poured and allowed to cool in the lipped bowl.

7 The tea is placed in the pot, using a scoop. The quantity depends on the quality of the tea and the number of people drinking. The delicacy of the taste of green tea means that the brew should not be too strong. The older traditions of Korean tea distinguish between the seasons here. The great 19th-century master, Cho Ui, indicated that the tea should be placed in the pot first, then the water poured on, only in winter (*Hatu-beop*), whereas in spring and autumn he was accustomed to half-filling the tea pot with water first, then adding the tea, before pouring in the rest of the water (*Chungtu-beop*); in summer, he suggested, the pot should be filled with water first, then the tea added (*Sangtu-beop*). He felt that these different methods ensured the best taste for the changing seasons. Today virtually everyone follows his winter method, without further thought.

8   When the water has cooled enough, it is gently poured into the pot. The tea is allowed to draw in the pot for a short while. The length of time needed for the tea to brew varies considerably but it should not usually exceed much more than a minute; only experience can serve as a reliable guide here. Occasionally, the first serving of a very fine tea is made with really cool water, which is kept on the leaves to draw for a longer time than otherwise. The resulting infusion can be amazingly rich in flavor; the hotter the water, the more quickly bitter tasting elements emerge, which easily dominate and suppress the other tastes.

9   The water used to warm the cups is poured away into the waste water bowl. A new measure of hot water may already be placed in the lipped bowl to cool for the second serving, if the water is very hot.

10   The first serving of tea is poured directly from the pot into the cups, which are arranged in a row before the person presiding, a little at a time, back and forward, in order to spread equally the stronger brew that emerges from the bottom of the teapot. No water must remain in the pot, or it would develop the bitter taste that is so undesirable.

11   The filled cups are put on the saucers and these are then moved to the part of the table directly in front of the guests. According to strict etiquette, cups should not be passed directly from hand to hand; only one person moving at a time is the rule. In very formal ceremonies, an assistant may carry the filled cups on a tray from the table where they are filled to the guests sitting on cushions some distance from the table.

12   Korean tea is usually drunk holding the cup in both hands. But when drinking informally, using just one hand is perfectly acceptable. The first step is to view the color of the tea, the second to inhale its fragrance, the third to taste it on the tongue, the fourth to follow its taste in the throat, and finally to enjoy the lingering aftertaste in the mouth. Tea is reckoned to contain five or six tastes: salt, sweet, bitter, tart, peppery, sour in varying proportions.

13   The water for brewing the second round is poured into the pot. It can be a little hotter than that used for the first. The leaves having softened, the water needs to stand on them for only a very short moment, then the tea is poured from the teapot into the lipped bowl. That is passed around, people serving themselves directly. This avoids passing cups back and forth. Sometimes one guest will offer to pour tea for the guests close by, the main thing is not to make much a fuss about it all.

Often, delicacies known as *chasik* are offered between the later cups of tea

14 Ordinary green tea will usually have lost most of its flavor after steeping three times, but very good tea may be used to make four or five rounds.

15 Often, delicacies known as *chasik* are offered between the later cups of tea; some of the most popular are small pastels made of pine-pollen or other fragrant natural substances, combined with a little honey. Rice cakes are also very popular, but these should not be too sweet or the delicate taste of the tea will be overwhelmed.

16 Once everyone has finished drinking, the cups are gathered together by the person presiding, who removes them from the saucers and arranges them in a row. In formal ceremonies, the tea in the pot is emptied into the large bowl, then the pot is rinsed and wiped. The cups are washed, wiped, turned upside down, then the cover is unfolded and laid on top of the tea set. In less formal settings, the washing up is done later in private. The used tea leaves can be employed in a variety of ways: in cooking, in bathwater or as a hair-rinse, or to remove the smell from a refrigerator.

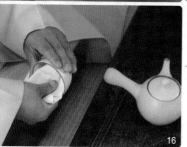

For people drinking tea alone, Korean potteries also now produce a wide variety of individual tea sets. These usually consist of a cup, a perforated sleeve or filter that fits inside the cup, and a lid. The tea leaves are placed inside the filter, well-below boiling temperature water is poured over them until the cup is nearly full, then the cup is covered with the lid for a minute or so. The lid is removed, placed upside-down on the table, and the filter slowly removed, allowing the brewed tea to drain completely into the cup. The filter is then placed on the upturned lid and the tea drunk. The filter can then be replaced and the process repeated. Other types of individual tea sets consist of a miniature pot with a lid and a lip for pouring, with a matching cup of the same size.

In place of a teapot, it is also possible to use one of the upright glass cylinders with a plunger that have become very popular for making coffee. Of course, tea should not be made in one that has already been used for coffee! Glass teapots are also popular now when making Chinese tea, and stores that sell Chinese tea wares usually stock a good variety of glass teapots and jugs. The glass offers the advantage of being able to appreciate fully the developing colors of different teas as they brew.

In the summer, it is possible to make a refreshing cold tea by placing tea leaves in a bottle of cold spring water and allowing them to steep overnight in the fridge. Likewise, tea can be placed in the water-bottle taken on walks, giving it time to steep before being drunk.

Whisked powdered tea

Sometimes powdered tea (*garu-cha* or *malcha*) is served in Korea, although far less frequently than in Japan. In this case, the tea is whisked with a delicate bamboo whisk (*cha-seon* or *chat-sol*) in a larger bowl (*chat sabal* or *chawan*) from which it is then drunk. The whisk is usually placed on a specially shaped pottery stand when not in use. This is the way Koreans used to drink tea in the Goryeo period (918-1392), following the method developed in China during the Sung Dynasty. In Japan, it has remained the normal form for the tea ceremony until today.

1   The bowl is first rinsed in hot water, to warm it, and the whisk is also rinsed in the water.

2   This water is poured off, and the bowl is dried with a small cloth.

3   The powdered tea is taken from its container on a long, thin bamboo spoon and tipped into the bowl. A first whipping brings up a froth.

4   More water is added and a final brisk whipping should develop a firm layer of froth across the whole surface of the tea. It is also possible to add the full quantity of water at the start.

5   The bowl is then presented to the guest, who drinks the contents in a series of sips.

6   Since this is a suspension of powdered leaves, a deposit may

remain at the bottom of the cup; usually a little extra water is poured into the cup, lightly swirled then drunk.

In Japan this is the kind of tea used for the formal tea ceremony and all kinds of complicated rules dictate every stage of the process, including turning the cup through 180 degrees before drinking, and consuming the tea in three mouthfuls. None of this is necessary when drinking powdered tea in Korea.

Powdered tea can also be drunk mixed with milk. In this case, the easiest method is to place it and the milk in a closed bottle and shake it vigorously. This is not traditional, but it makes a very pleasant cool drink in summer.

Some Korean Tea Poems

North, south, the mountain is
sliced by slivers of tracks;
raindrops, heavy with pine pollen,
fall dizzily down.
The hermit draws water and
returns to his straw hut;
soon a ribbon of blue smoke dyes
the white clouds.

Yi Sung-in (1349‑1392)

I sit alone, deep in the mountains:
Worldly affairs are of no import.
Gate closed, I pass the days
in learning emptiness.
I examine my life.
I have no material goods,
just a bowl of fresh tea and
a book of scriptures.

The Ven. Sonsu (1543˜1614)

It's never been possible
to fabricate nature.
Why do I look for enlightenment outside?
All I know for truth is that
there is no action in the heart.
Thirsty, I brew tea;
tired, I take a nap.

The Ven. Hyegun (1320˜1376)

This year I am debilitated
by sickness racked by thirst.
My only joy is the odd bowl of tea.
In the clear dawn I draw
tingling cold spring water;
I brew at my leisure the golden
"Dewdrop Leaf" in a stoneware pot.

Seo Ko-jeong (1420-1488)

The exotic pomegranate,
a flame on the green branch,
is reflected on the white curtain
with the passing afternoon sun.
The brazier burns itself out,
the tea bubbles;
a perfect time for the hermit
to unroll a painting.

Yi Tok-mu (1741-1793)

An anecdote for every bowl.
Gradually we approached the mystery.
The joy is limpid, plain.
Does one have to be tipsy to be drunk?

Yi Gyu-bo (1168 1241)

Five tea poems by Cho Ui, translated by Ven. Jineul

I

At Tochon's place, where he practices Seon and takes his ease,
the mind becomes distant, and days go slowly.
A path leads to stone steps around hidden orchids;
a gate faces rocky peaks beyond a curved pond.
He decocts herb medicine to disperse ennui,
he drinks tea to reduce sleep.
A past promise to live with rosy clouds
comes true naturally in the clear autumn.

2

To listen to the songs of birds, I skipped the evening meditation,
enjoyed a patch of grass by the edge of an ancient mountain stream.
Pleasure recollected depends on a beautiful phrase;
the appreciative mind meets with a close friend.
Spring water cries out in a rocky valley;
pine trees echo when wind is coming.
I drank a cup of tea and watched the flowing and stillness.
Quietly and naturally I seemed to forget the return of time.

3

Here the sky's light is like water and water is like mist.
I came and enjoyed it here; now already a half-year has passed.
Good nights were like lying down under a bright moon;
a clear river is now facing white sea gulls sleeping.
Since hatred and jealousy have not stayed in my mind,
how could either discredit or honor approach the rim of my ear?
In my sleeve there still remains some Enlightening Thunder Smile tea.
Drifting like a cloud, I will try the spring water at Turung again.

4

The new moon is beautiful in the sky in early evening.
Clear light shining amiably is boundless.
A group of stars circle clearly around the Milky Way.
All come together with Jade Dew tea and make a sleepless night.

5

From long ago, saints and sages have both loved tea.
Tea is like a perfect gentleman whose nature has no evil.
The first human had tea in earliest times
when he entered far into Snowy Mountain to pick tea leaves.
Thereafter its qualities have been transmitted by the Way of Tea
and teas were kept in jade jars like ten kinds of brocade.
After long seeking, the best water for tea was found in the Yellow River
which has eight kinds of virtue and also beauty.

Water should be drawn from the depths and examined for lightness
and softness.
If water is really pure, it develops both the body and the spirit of the tea.
When all dirt and coarseness are eliminated
and essential vitality enters,
attainment of the Great Path is not far off, is it?
When I pay homage to the Spiritual Mountain and
offer tea to all Buddhas,
I must be careful of the boiling point and consider Buddhist precepts.
Although the real body of Och-ieh tea seeks its mysterious origin,
the mysterious origin is the Perfection of Non-Attachment.
Alas, I was born three thousand years after the Buddha;
his voice is dim as the Sound of the Tide from the primordial heaven.
I wanted to seek the mysterious origin but obtained nothing.
I deeply regret that I was not born before the Buddha left the world.
So far I have not been able to wash away my love of tea,
so I brought some to the Eastern Land (Korea) to smile
at my difficulty.
I'm now unpacking the brocade wrappings from a jade jar,
to make a gift of some tea to close friends first.

A few stanzas from Cho Ui's *Dongdasong* (Hymns to Korean Tea) translated by Ven. Jineul

How can I teach the wonderful functions of tea, with its nine difficulties and four fragrances,
to the Seon practitioners sitting in the Jade Pavilion at Chilbul Temple in Jiri Mountain?
If the nine difficulties are overcome, the four sorts of fragrance will develop fully.
Its perfect taste can be presented as an offering within the nine walls of the royal palace.

When tea's blue waves and green fragrance enter the court of the heart,
intelligence and brightness reach everywhere unimpeded.
Then your spiritual roots will rest on divine mountains,
though in appearance immortals seem a different species.

Mysterious delicacy lies at the center, hard to express.
True essence should not be divided into body and spirit, water and tea.
Body and spirit must be equal, without loss of what is fair and appropriate.
What is fair and appropriate is no different from the combined health and

subtlety of tea.

When I drink a cup of Jade Flower tea, a wind rises under my arms,
my body grows light and I ascend to a state of purity.
The bright moon becomes my candle, my friend,
while white clouds offer me a seat and set up a screen.

Bamboo sounds and pine tree waves together cool me;
clean cold air penetrates my bones, awakens my mind.
I still like a white cloud and the bright moon to be my guests.
Where a Man of the Way sits, those are enough.

The other poems above and in the previous section are taken from "The Poetry of Tea"
by Chung Min. *Koreana*. Winter 1997. Volume 11, Number 4.
http://eng.actakoreana.org/clickkorea/text/10-Ceramic/10-97win-poetry.html

The Virtues of Tea

Early in the Joseon period, a scholar named Yi Mok (1471-1498) wrote a book about tea, titled *Chabu* (On Tea), in which he made the following claims:

Tea has five functions

> It quenches thirst.
> It consoles the lonely heart.
> It draws host and guests closer together.
> It ensures good digestion.
> It relieves a hangover.

Tea has six virtues

> It bestows long life.
> It heals disease.
> It cheers the spirits.

It soothes the heart.

It purifies the mind.

It bestows propriety.

Why else, you may ask, would anyone drink expensive green tea? Preparing it seems so complicated, compared to a spoonful of instant coffee, or a tea bag, even one with uncertain contents. The most common answer given in Asia is always, not surprisingly perhaps, "because it is good for you." There are a number of pages on the Internet that list the following claims:

Green tea enhances health

Green tea prevents cancer

Green tea restricts the increase of blood cholesterol

Green tea controls high blood pressure

Green tea lowers the blood sugar level

Green tea suppresses aging

Green tea refreshes the body

Green tea deters food poisoning

Green tea stops cavities

Green tea fights viruses

Green tea acts as a functional food

In order to justify these claims, some web pages offer lists of the main components of green tea, together with a list of the healthy

effects of each. The great heroes are the Catechins, the main component in tea, it seems, which thanks to them is said to offer the following advantages: tea reduces the incidence of cancer, reduces tumors, reduces mutations, reduces oxidation by active oxygen, lowers blood cholesterol, inhibits increase of blood pressure, inhibits increase of blood sugar, kills bacteria, kills the influenza virus, fights cariogenic bacteria, prevents halitosis. Another hero is caffeine which, as we all know, stimulates wakefulness and also acts as a diuretic. In other words, too much green tea late in the evening is likely to keep you awake.

Other powerful components in a cup of tea include vitamins C, B and E, to say nothing of flavonoids that strengthen the blood vessel walls, polysaccharides that lower blood sugar, and fluorides that prevent dental cavities. Theanine (a kind of amino acid) closes the list and it comes as rather a surprise to read that it simply "gives green tea its delicious taste." After all, medicine surely ought not to have a delicious taste? In any case, green tea is certainly better for one than any other kind of drink.

These claims are not in themselves new. In Japan's Kamakura era (1191-1333), the monk Eisai stressed the beneficial effects of tea in his book *Kissa Yojoki* (*The medical benefits of drinking tea*, 1211): "Tea is a miraculous medicine for the maintenance of health. Tea has an extraordinary power to prolong life. Anywhere a person cultivates tea, long life will follow. In ancient and modern times, tea is the elixir that creates the mountain-dwelling immortal."

We might also quote the words of Lu Yu near the beginning of the *Classic of Tea*: "If one is generally moderate but is feeling hot or warm, given to melancholia, suffering from aching of the brain, smarting of the eyes, troubled in the four limbs or afflicted in the hundred joints, he may take tea four or five time. Its liquor is like the sweetest dew of Heaven." That is not so far from one modern British term for tea: "The Cup that Cheers," and certainly many housewives would echo that bit about the hundred aching joints.

This preoccupation with the physical benefits derived from what we eat and drink is a familiar one in China as well as Korea. It certainly appeals to many people in the whole world today, in the name of "well-being." Yet this hardly offers a full or sufficient explanation of how we should approach tea. Generally speaking, most people's main category for evaluating food and drink remains gustatory pleasure, the criteria are basically aesthetic. After all, "It's good for you," is something we tell children when we want them to eat food that they do not enjoy.

But traditionally, tea-drinking in Asia has a philosophical side to it that demands training and sophistication. Lu Yu, in his *Classic of Tea*, noted that "when one devotes oneself to tea and steeps oneself in wisdom, moral principles and virtue; when one cultivates one's nature through tea and develops good behavior, thinks about existence, meditates and searches for truth, so as to find spiritual well-being and moral purity, then one attains the superior kingdom of tea: the Way of Tea."

One very well-known expression of the Way of Tea comes from Lu Tung, a poet of the Chinese T'ang Dynasty:

The first bowl moistens my lips and throat;
The second bowl banishes all loneliness;
The third bowl clears my mind of words and books.
At the fourth cup, I begin to perspire and
life's troubles evaporate through my pores.
The fifth cup cleanses my entire being.
Six cups and I am in the realm of the Divine.
Seven cups - ah, but I can drink no more:
I can only feel the gentle breeze blowing through my sleeves,
wafting me away to the Isle of Immortality!

The Korean Way of Tea

Much of what is said about tea by some of its Korean adepts likewise suggests a sublime level of approach, not just health or pleasure. The Way of Tea is presented as nothing less than a spiritual, religious activity leading to higher levels of inner awakening, if not total enlightenment. The great tea master Chae Won-Hwa, who heads the Panyaro Institute for the Way of Tea in Seoul, teaches what she received from her master, the Venerable Hyodang Choi Beom-Sul:

The Panyaro Seon (Zen) of Tea

The Way of Tea takes the simple, everyday gestures of making and drinking tea and makes of them a spiritual way. The Seon (Zen) of Tea suggests that in drinking tea in such a manner, one touches the edge of an intuitive meditation:

Seon is a reality that can never be explained in words or writing.
Seon is concentration, a positive awareness.
Seon is above all free and creative, and subjective too.
Seon offers a shortcut by which to reach a limitless individuality.
Just like tea.
All you need to do is prepare tea and savor on the tip of your tongue its six tastes: bitter, tart, sour, salt, spicy-hot, and sweet.
Tea and Seon should constantly govern and guide both body and mind; only so can such a level be attained.
Therefore people have said, "tea and Seon have a single taste," and also, "tea and Seon are one."

Reflecting this approach, she lists a variety of ways of celebrating the Way of Tea:

Seon tea ceremony with several participants
Sitting meditating in a tea room, hearing the light murmur of the water boiling on a charcoal fire, the master and disciples prepare and drink tea together in the proper manner, either powdered tea

or leaf tea: a Seon of Tea that instructs both body and mind.

Tea ceremony to welcome guests
The master carefully prepares tea and offers it to guests: a Seon of Tea that instructs by a shared drinking of tea.

Ceremony offering tea to Buddha, to spirits or to ancestors
This solemn ceremony marks the end of an eventful year; candles are lit late in a night bright with stars, and the tea that is prepared is offered on the altar to the spirits above, all sensing the approach of a new year, bright with new hope.

Seon tea ceremony with a single celebrant
Alone, the master prepares and drinks tea, deep in meditation: the Seon of Tea at its deepest, most universal.

A Brief History of
Tea in China

The raw leaves of the wild tea trees found in the southwestern regions of what is now China were surely used to make a healing, soothing drink from very early times. In Chinese legend, or myth, the qualities of tea are said to have been first discovered by the Second Emperor, Shen Nung (the Divine Healer, reputed to have reigned 2737- 2697 B.C.), who was also said to have discovered millet, medicinal herbs, and to have invented the plough. His predecessor, Fu Hsi, the First Emperor, had given humanity knowledge of fire, cooking, and music, while the Third Emperor completed the Promethean task of human happiness by revealing the secrets of the vine and astronomy.

There is an early Chinese text of 50 B.C. that mentions tea being prepared by servants. Certainly tea was being cultivated in

Szechuan by the third century of our era. The first detailed description of tea-drinking is found in the ancient Chinese dictionary mentioned below, dating from before 350. At this time the fresh green leaves were picked, then pressed to form "bricks" that were roasted to a reddish hue. These were crumbled into water and boiled with the addition of onion, ginger, and orange to give a kind of herbal soup that must have been very bitter but was considered to be good as a remedy for stomach problems, bad eyesight, and many other diseases.

In 519 the great Indian master Bodhidharma, the traditional founder of the "Seon (Zen)" school of Buddhism, came to China. The Japanese sometimes claim that he brought tea with him from India, which seems most unlikely since there seems to be no record of people in India knowing how to make a drink using their own tea trees until the 19th century. Another story says that when he found himself growing weary after staying awake for seven years, Bodhidharma plucked off his eyelids. He threw them to the ground and two tea trees sprang up, that had the power to keep him awake and alert. There is certainly an ancient Buddhist tradition of drinking tea before an image of Bodhidharma.

The Names for Tea

Originally, the Chinese had no separate ideogram for "tea." The earliest texts used a variety of characters that are also the names of other plants. The most ancient and most frequently used character is 茶, pronounced *t'u*, which was the name of the bitter-tasting sow thistle. Poem 35 in the *Shi Jing* (*Book of Odes / Songs*), which was written at the very latest in the 6th century B.C. reads: "who says the sowthistle (*t'u*) is bitter? It is as sweet as the shepherd's purse." Around 50 B.C. Wang Piu wrote of buying *t'u* from Wutu, a mountain in the Szechuan tea growing district. Four centuries later Emperor Ai Ti's father-in-law Wang Mang was an advocate of *t'u*: "fragrant *t'u* dominates the six passions. The taste for it spreads over the entire Kingdom." Probably these texts mostly refer to our tea plant. Another character used was that for the catalpa tree, pronounced *kia* or *chia*. This is found in a revision of the ancient Chinese dictionary *Kuo P'o* dated 265-317, that specifies: "A beverage is made from the leaves by boiling. Now the earliest gathering is called *t'u* and the latest *ming*." *Ming* was another early name used for tea. It reached Yunnan (southwestern China) from the word *miang* of the Siamese Hakka dialect. The mythical Emperor Shen Nung, also known as the Divine Husbandsman, was said to have discovered tea when a leaf fell into his cup of boiled water around 2,737 B.C. The earliest accounts of that legend, dating from the Han Dynasty (206-220 A.D.), use the word *ming*.

These assorted characters with multiple meanings led to much confusion. Some of the ambiguity is said to have been eliminated when an emperor in the Han Dynasty ruled that the character *t'u* should be pronounced *cha* when referring to tea. Finally, sometime

in the eighth century, the character was simplified into 茶 by removing the horizontal bar at the top of the vertical stroke and this became the generally accepted character for tea after it was used by Lu Yu in his *Classic of Tea* (*Cha Ching*) in 780. It has always been pronounced *cha* or *chai* throughout almost the whole of China, but in the language used in Fujian province, around the port of Amoy, a "t" took the place of the initial "ch" and so we find the variant pronunciations *ta* or *tai*. The earliest suppliers of tea to the Dutch and English traders in Indonesia came from Amoy and taught them the name in their pronunciation, with an initial "t." Thanks to them, "tea" is the form of name also used in other European countries such as France or Germany.

In contrast, when tea was exported along the Silk Road to Persia and Turkey, then later as far as Russia, and down into the Indian subcontinent, it came bearing the usual Chinese name of *cha* or *chai*, by which it is still known in those regions, and in fact the Portuguese who first established direct trading relations with China also knew it with that pronunciation. In Korea today we find both pronunciations being used almost interchangeably, *cha* and *ta*, just as the quotations from the early years of tea in Europe show that at the beginning people spoke of both *cha* and *tay*. It is still possible to hear British people talking of "a nice cup of char." However, that pronunciation may have been reintroduced to London by cockney sailors from the 19th-century tea clippers, who had heard it used in the Chinese ports where they collected their cargo.

The character 茶 combines three simple characters. At the top is that for "grass" and at the bottom that for "tree," with between them the character for "man," and it is often said to symbolize in that way a harmony between human beings and the world of nature.

The development of tea-drinking

A major turning-point in the history of tea came in the 8th century, with the composition of the *Classic of Tea* (*Cha Ching*) by Lu Yu in 780, which summarizes everything known at that time about every aspect of tea growing and preparation. This book seems to have been commissioned by the tea merchants of the time to give a new impetus to the consumption of tea by the upper classes. It certainly succeeded. The crumbled cakes (or "bricks") of tea were now boiled with nothing but a little salt and this was the form of tea that became the national drink of the elite in China's T'ang Dynasty (618-907). Moreover, since this kind of tea could be transported easily, a taste for it began to spread far beyond China, into Tibet, along the Silk Road to Turkey and India, and ultimately into Russia where the samovar was duly invented to facilitate tea-drinking by providing hot water at any time.

Lu Yu's influence was enormous. He was the first to suggest that the ritual of preparing and drinking tea represented a code of symbolic harmony and order reflecting the ideals of cosmos and society. In his *Classic of Tea*, Lu Yu lists no less than twenty-four implements that are essential for the correct preparation of a cup of tea. These include the equipment needed for roasting and grinding the cakes of tea, as well as the stove for boiling the water, and the cups for drinking. Rich noblemen at once began to rival one another in acquiring beautifully crafted sets for making tea, while tea plantations spread across the southern part of China. The bricks of tea were crushed to a powder which was tipped into boiling water in a cauldron, from where the tea was poured frothing into bowls.

By 850 people were also beginning to dry tea in the form of detached leaves, not compressed into bricks. A great change came with the transition to the Sung Dynasty (960-1279), when Chinese culture reached a new summit of refinement. Tea now began to be drunk in a form familiar to many from the Japanese tea ceremony, for which dried blocks of green tea are ground to a fine powder. This is mixed with hot water directly in the bowls, whipped to a froth with a bamboo whisk.

The finest tea of the Sung Dynasty was produced in the imperial plantations in Fujian, molded into blocks stamped with dragon designs, and sent to the capital as imperial tribute. Such tea was treated with great respect, it was wrapped in silk and bamboo leaves, and carried in precious caskets with golden locks. The tea in these blocks was normally perfumed with essences of camphor, musk, or other spices, although the people in the tea-producing regions usually drank unperfumed tea. One writer (Chou Mi) claimed that "one measure of tea requires 400,000 leaves. Yet, this

is barely enough to make a few cups to sip."

Tea culture reached new heights under the emperor Hui-tsung (1101-1126), an aesthete who was untiring in his search for new varieties of tea and qualities of taste. He particularly liked an unperfumed "white tea" of great rarity and from his time the use of perfumes in tea was largely abandoned. Meanwhile, the appreciation of leaf tea had spread far and wide among the literati. It too was usually ground to a powder and whisked in the bowls, much like the brick tea.

Then came the Mongols. Genghis Khan conquered Beijing in 1215, his grandson was Kublai Khan who overthrew the southern Sung in 1279. The Mongols liked to put cream in a boil-up of old-fashioned brick tea, which they consumed rather like soup during meals. Kublai Khan founded the Yuan Dynasty (1279-1367) and it was at this time that Marco Polo claimed to have visited China, and wrote Europe's first report about the country, without ever mentioning tea! Yet the drinking of powdered tea continued to be immensely popular through the Yuan and into the Ming Dynasty (1368-1644).

The Ming Dynasty (1368-1644), that followed the Yuan, set out to restore earlier Chinese ways in a cultural renaissance. The founder of the new dynasty, Chu Yuan-chang (reigned 1368-1399) was a man of humble origins who enjoyed drinking leaf tea and promoted tea production. In 1391 he decreed that brick tea should no longer be produced, and that all tribute tea should be leaf tea. The production of cake (brick) tea for the imperial court had been a highly complex and very expensive process, an extravagant source of corruption and waste. Once such tea was no longer available, the ritual of preparing whisked tea from powdered tea was quickly abandoned by literati in most of China. Chinese society was becoming increasingly commercial. There were more and more wealthy merchants who wished to practice cultivated pursuits, including tea-drinking in elegant surroundings. Eventually commercial tea-rooms were opened in the towns to accommodate them.

It was during the Ming Dynasty that the method of allowing the tea leaves to soak (steep) in hot water for a time before drinking the infusion became general. This produces a transparent infusion, whereas powdered tea contains the actual leaves. The Ming aesthetes continued to look for the "true flavor" of tea, as before, by this new method. The result was a proliferation of drying methods, some rapid and some slow, that each resulted in a distinct kind of tea. The many kinds of "oolong" tea, now the most characteristic form of Chinese tea, date from this period. Writers praised the tea from particular sites, and recommended using the water from specific wells to make them. Every aspect of tea preparation became an object of connoisseurship. During the later Ming, literati came to prefer white porcelain for teacups, since it best allowed the color of the tea to be admired. The art of tea was by this time virtually complete, and every true connoisseur had his tea room, located in an attractive spot near his library and study, equipped with beautiful utensils, often of considerable antiquity, where he could offer a variety of exquisite teas to his discerning friends.

A History of Tea
in Korea

K orean tea-drinking is often said to have begun in prehistoric
times with "*Baeksan cha*" (White Mountain tea), a drink
made using the tender spring leaves of a tree of the azalea family
native to the highlands of Mount Baekdu, on the present frontier
between China and North Korea. A well-known legend claims that
green tea was first brought to Korea early in the 2nd century of the
current era by a princess from Ayodhya in India who married King
Suro, the first king of Garak, a small kingdom at the far south-east
tip of the peninsula. Other legends link the introduction of tea to
the foundation of the earliest Buddhist temples, either Bulgap-sa (in
Yonggwang) and Bulhui-sa (in Naju) around 384, or that of
Hwaeom-sa (in Gurye) in 544. Certainly the drinking of tea seems
to have been current by the sixth or seventh centuries, probably

introduced and fostered by Buddhist monks returning from China, where the many schools of Buddhism attracted some of Korea's finest scholars.

There are reports in the early chronicle-histories known as *Samguk-yusa* and *Samguk-sagi* that Queen Sondeok of Silla (ruled 632-47) drank tea and that King Munmu (ruled 661-81) in 661 ordered tea to be used during ceremonial offerings in honor of King Suro of Garak. King Sinmun (ruled 681-92) advocated the use of tea in order to purify the mind, while King Heungdeok (ruled 826-36) is reported to have received tea seeds from T'ang China which he ordered to be planted on Jiri Mountain in 828. Today, there are two modern monuments celebrating this event, near Hwaeom-sa and Ssanggye-sa, the two temples that both claim to have been the site of that first planting; but of course in actual fact these may not have been the first tea seeds planted Korea. However, in Japan, the first record of brick tea being used dates from around 593, and the first planting of seeds is said to have occurred in 805, giving a very similar chronology.

Other early indications of the growing significance of tea in Korea include a report that King Honan (ruled 857-861) sent a gift of tea and incense to the Ven. Sucheol's memorial service. Chungdam, a monk and poet who lived during the reign of King Gyeongdeok (ruled 742-765), is said to have started the tradition of Buddhist tea rituals by making regular offerings of tea to the Maitreya, the Buddha of the Future, on Mount Namsan in

Gyeongju. There are also records that renowned Silla scholars such as Seol Chong and Choe Chi-won drank tea.

By the Goryeo Dynasty (918-1392), the culture of tea was at its height and it was the subject of some of Korea's oldest recorded poems. The royal palace developed an elaborate ritual for drinking tea. An office called the "Tabang" (Tea Chamber) was established to officiate over tea rites at important national events. The tea ceremony in the court was an extremely elaborate ritual accompanied by music; pavilions and arbors were built for tea parties and poetry readings with court officials. Scholar-officials had their own way of enjoying tea, which was leisurely and relaxed, often taking the form of parties at scenic locations with music, dance, and poetry. Likewise ceremonies known as *Heon-cha* were widely held, in which cups of green tea were offered before the statues of the Buddha in the temples. Because tea was believed to help monks meditate, their tea-drinking was known as *sammae* (*samdhi*, spiritual concentration) style. Tea was also widely offered in ancestral ceremonies, which are still today known as *Cha-rye* (tea rituals), although tea has not usually been offered in them during recent centuries. It seems clear that much of the finest Goryeo pottery was made for use in tea ceremonies of various kinds.

The culture of tea in Korea was originally identified with Buddhism. However, when Buddhism was replaced by Confucianism as the main official religious tradition after Joseon took over from the Goryeo Dynasty at the end of the 14th century, and most temples were destroyed, the drinking of tea continued. Many monks became hermits and developed their own tea tradition, which came to be known as "hermit tea art." In the meantime, the founding fathers of the new dynasty adopted tea drinking as a part of their official daily routine. According to the "bureaucratic tea art," officials met over tea every day to discuss government affairs. Auditors from the Office of the Inspector General had nighttime tea sessions when they investigated corrupt officials. There were special employees who served tea at such meetings, and their titles varied according to the rank of the officials they served. A eunuch was responsible for serving tea to the king.

In the 1590s, the Japanese invaded Korea and forced hundreds of the best Korean potters to go and work in Japan. Many of the finest bowls used in Japanese tea ceremonies were made in Korea or were produced in Japan by potters of Korean descent. In the time prior to and even following the

immensely destructive Japanese invasion, that was ultimately thwarted, tea still played a major role in Korean culture at the highest levels. But the taxes payable on tea production became so excessive that many tea fields were destroyed, tea became a rare and highly-priced commodity.

Finally, King Yeongjo (ruled 1724-1776) ordered that wine or boiled water should be served in its place. From then on, wine was used instead of tea for offerings in most rituals, including ancestral rites, and water took the place of tea before the statues in temples. Though waning, the tea tradition managed to survive in a limited way. The court continued to observe a special tea ritual based on the *Kukcho oryeui* (Five Rites of State) that had been compiled in 1474 as guidelines for conducting major state ceremonies. Upper-class families held tea rites during coming-of-age, wedding, funeral and memorial ceremonies in the manner prescribed in *Sarye pyeollam* (Handbook of Four Rites), and a few

Buddhist monks continued tea rituals established by such famed masters as Sosan (1520-1604) and Baekpa (1767-1852). Tea thus survived as ritual rather than as ordinary practice. That tea continued to be drunk socially in some circles during the later years of the Joseon Dynasty is shown by the following story.

At the start of our 19th century, the young scholar Jeong Yak-yong (1762-1836) found himself exiled from Seoul and obliged to live in a poor inn in his mother's hometown of Gangjin, in the far southwest of the country. One day in 1805, when he was in his fourth year of exile and desperate for some intelligent conversation, he heard that an educated monk of good family was in charge of Paengnyeon-sa Temple, less than ten miles away. He duly went to meet the Venerable Hyejang (1772-1811), who introduced him to tea. The monk soon enabled the exiled scholar to move into a building forming part of Goseong-sa Temple just outside of Gangjin. A little later, the local people helped him move to a small house on the slopes of a nearby hill where many wild tea trees grew, known as Dasan (Tea Mountain), and Dasan became the name by which Jeong Yak-yong is usually referred to. He cultivated the Way of Tea and taught it to the young men who came to be taught by him there. They formed a little organization among themselves, known as the *Dasingye* (Tea Lovers' Society).

Hyejang expressed the Way of Tea in one of his poems:

I climb to the top of the hill

and pluck some tea leaves;
I let the water in
and irrigate the flower patch.
I turn my head. Today's sun
already is low on the mountain.
Wind-bells echo from
a distant hermitage;
crows roost in an old tree.
Oh joy! Such ease,
such pleasure, such beauty!

In 1809, a young Buddhist monk, Cho Ui (1786-1866), visited Dasan and stayed with him for several months, learning from him about tea. Recognized in Korea as the great restorer of the Way of Tea in 19th-century Korea, Cho Ui later built the hermitage known as Ilchi-am above the temple called Daeheung-sa near Haenam, in the far south of Korea, and lived there for many years, cultivating the Way of Tea in his own tea-room. The story of Cho Ui's tea-friendship with the famous scholar and calligrapher Kim Jeong-hui, better known as Chusa, is especially touching. From 1840 until 1848, Chusa was exiled to the southern island of Jeju and during those years Cho Ui visited him no less than five times, once staying for six months, bringing him gifts of tea and practicing Buddhist meditation together. Cho Ui's close relationship with him and many of his scholar friends was very unusual at the time, for most

Confucian gentlemen tended to despise Buddhist monks; tea played an important role in their relations, with gifts of tea acknowledged by formal tea poems. Here is one poem written by Chusa:

> I sit here quietly, tea half drunk,
> flavor as the first.
> The mystery unfolds
> waters flow, flowers burst.

Yet despite the efforts of Cho Ui, the Way of Tea remained almost unknown in Korea, except among monks. In 1910, after years of gradual encroachment, Japan finally annexed the Korean nation, and exercised close control over every aspect of its life until Liberation came with the Japanese surrender at the end of the Pacific War in 1945. Every aspect of traditional Korean life and culture was viewed as suspect and much was actively suppressed; Korean history was replaced by Japanese history, and in later years in schools Korea's children were forced to study, and only speak, Japanese as their "national language." Since Japan was intensely proud of its own tea tradition, there was no room for a rival, or alternative Korean tea tradition and tea-making of the traditional kind became even rarer.

Then, after Liberation in 1945, the destruction and poverty caused by the Korean War (1950-53) left people with little room to think about tea-drinking. The restoration of a specifically Korean Way of Tea in the course of recent decades was due in large part to the efforts of a group of people who gathered around the Venerable Hyodang, Choi Beom-sul (1904 - 1979). For many years he was head monk of Dasol-sa Temple near Jinju, to the southeast of Jiri Mountain. He is often considered to have been the Cho Ui of the 20th century, for he wrote the first full length study of tea to be published in modern Korea, *Hangukui Chado* (*The Korean Way of Tea*, 1973), and introduced many people from all walks of life to the Korean tradition of tea. He was active in the Korean Independence Movement during the Japanese colonial period (1910 - 1945), and founded several schools and universities, as well as being the teacher of virtually all the leading figures in the modern Korean tea revival. Early in 1977, he organized the Korean Association for the Way of Tea (*Hanguk Chado-hoi*) at Tasol-sa and in 1978, the *Cha-Seon-hoi* (Tea-Zen Association) was established in Seoul. However, these early associations did not survive his death in 1979.

Today there exist a complicated variety of tea associations in Korea, many founded in recent years, often centered on one particular tea master and with an outreach limited to one particular city or region. Their activities may have some degree of success but they often lack any concrete link with the actual making of tea in springtime, or with the wider, deeper literary and spiritual tea traditions that Hyodang so often stressed. The popularity of tea has been encouraged by regional "tea festivals" in the main production areas, and by the promulgation of a "National Tea Day" in May.

Meanwhile, Hyodang's widow, Chae Won-Hwa, has ensured a full transmission and continuation of all the aspects of the Way of Tea that she learned from Hyodang. She established the Panyaro Institute for the Way of Tea in the Insa-dong neighborhood of Seoul on July 2, 1983, in accordance with Hyodang's wishes. She has now been instructing members in the Way of Tea known as *Seon-cha* (Zen-tea) for over twenty years. Recently she, and other tea masters, too, have begun to demonstrate the Korean Way of Tea during cultural events held outside of Korea, to great effect.

An increasing number of Korean potters have begun to make tea sets, usually as part of a more general revival of rustic style handcrafted stoneware for domestic use. At the same time, since the mid-1980s "traditional tea rooms" have opened in the major cities, where good green tea and other teas are served. Usually, they also sell boxes of tea, tea sets and other objects related to traditional tea culture, which are otherwise not easily available.

Many middle and high schools encourage their students to

prepare green tea in the traditional manner, as part of a more general initiation into Korea's traditional culture, although this depends on the availability of someone on the staff able to teach tea. However, unlike in Taiwan, there has until very recently been little commercial interest in creating new ways of using green tea. The recent craze in Taiwan for tea rooms offering younger customers a variety of "bubble teas" or "tea cocktails" and other innovations has had almost no impact in Korea. Still, with an increase in ecological awareness and thanks to a craze for "well-being" it is now possible to eat green-tea ice-cream, drink a variety of green-tea flavored soft drinks from cans and plastic bottles, and eat green-tea cakes and bread. Green tea is also beginning to make its appearance in ecologically-oriented cosmetics and health products.

Some of the above information is taken from an anonymous web page: http://www.harvestfields.ca/Tea/Info/history_korean.htm

How Tea Came to the West

The first reference to China's tea known in a European text dates from 1559, when the Italian geographer Giovanni Battista Ramusio mentioned "*chai*" in his collection of other people's reports about Asia forming the second volume of his *Delle navigatione et viaggi*. In 1598, a London printer published an English translation of a Dutch navigator's account of his travels, *Iohn Huighen van Linschoten : his discours of voyages into ye Easte & West Indies* and that book contains the first use in English of the word for tea, as "*chaa*."

Tea itself first reached Western Europe from China early in the 17th century, initially imported by the Dutch via their settlements in Indonesia. The first known reference to tea by an Englishman dates from 1615, when a certain Richard Wickham, an agent of England's East India Company, wrote from Japan to a colleague in Macao asking to be sent "a pot of the best sort of chaw."

England's East India Company also began by purchasing tea from the Chinese merchants trading in the Dutch ports of Java; after 1686, when the British were expelled from Java, Chinese boats brought tea to Madras and Surat in India for sale to British merchants, but soon the English began to ship tea directly from the Chinese port of Amoy, in Fujian, and other ports on the mainland.

In the early London newspaper *Mercurius Politicus*, No. 435, of September 1658, the following advertisement appeared: "That excellent and by all Physicians approved China Drink called by the Chineans Tcha, by other nations *Tay*, alias Tee, is sold at the Sultaness Head, a cophee-house in Sweetings Rents, by the Royal Exchange, London." Thomas Garway, the first English tea dealer, and founder of the well-known coffeehouse, Garraway's, wrote a broadsheet, *An Exact Description of the Growth, Quality and Virtues of the Leaf Tea*, issued in 1659 or 1660: "in respect of its scarceness and dearness, it hath been only used as a *regalia* in high treatments and entertainments, and presents made thereof to princes and grandees." He offered it to the public, in the leaf, at fixed prices varying from 15 shillings to 50 shillings the pound, according to quality, and also in the infusion, "made according to the directions of the most knowing merchants and travelers into those eastern countries."

On September 25, 1660, the diarist Samuel Pepys noted, "I did send for a cup of tee, a China drink, of which I never had drunk before." In 1664 the East India Company presented King Charles

II with just over 2 pounds of "*thea*," which cost 40 shillings per pound, and two years afterwards with another parcel containing 224 pounds, for which the directors paid 50 shillings per pound. Both parcels appear to have been purchased from traders in Europe. Not until 1677 is the Company recorded to have taken any steps for the direct importation of tea. The order then given to their agents was for "teas of the best kind to the amount of 100 dollars." But the market soon grew and in 1703 orders were given for "75,000 pounds of Singlo (green), 10,000 pounds of Imperial, and 20,000 pounds of Bohea." The average price of tea at this period was 16 shillings per pound. As the 18th century progressed the use of tea in England rapidly increased, and by the close of the century the rate of consumption exceeded an average of 2 pounds per person per year.

(Portions of the above text are taken from the article on tea found in the 1911 edition of the *Encyclopedia Britannica*. There were 20 shillings in one pound sterling. In weight, just over 2 pounds correspond to 1 kilogram.)

The first detailed study of tea published in Europe was written by Dr. Wilhelm ten Rhyne (1649-1700), a celebrated Dutch physician and botanist who also wrote the first account of acupuncture. He lived in the Dutch "factory" (trading post) on the artificial island of Deshima in the harbor at Nagasaki (Japan) from 1674 to 1676. His text on tea, written in Latin, was published in Danzig in 1678, as an appendix to Jacob Breyn's *Exoticarum*

plantarum centuria prima (First Century of Exotic Plants).

Some years later, in 1683, the great German scholar Engelbert Kaempfer set out on a journey through Russia, Persia, Arabia and India. From there he sailed to Java, Siam, and finally Japan, where he lived for a time on Deshima island before returning to Europe in 1693. Kaempfer wrote his own account of Japanese tea to complement that of "my much honored friend" ten Rhyne. It was published in the third fascicle of his *Amoenitates Exoticae* (Exotic Pleasures, 1712). It covers every aspect of tea growing, making, and brewing. Kaempfer's work in making tea in Japan, and especially its botany, known in Europe, was hailed by the great botanist Linnaeus. The first edition of Linnaeus's *Species Plantarum* published in 1753 suggested calling the tea plant *Thea sinensis*, taking the Latin name for tea from Kaempfer and adding the Latin name for "Chinese."

The Chinese tea sold in Europe was divided between green tea and black tea (the latter often called "bohea"). A rather fanciful English writer of the mid-18th century, John Hill, declared in his *Treatise on Tea* (1753), quite without proof, that they came from different varieties of plant. Linnaeus in the second edition of his *Species* duly distinguished between *Thea viridis* (green) and *Thea bohea* (black). Neither Kaempfer nor Linnaeus seem to have suspected that there might be a link between *Thea* and the genus later named *Camellia* after a Moravian Jesuit called Kamel who studied Asian plants.

Early in the 19th century, tea seeds were obtained by stealth from China, after the English decided to challenge China's monopoly by trying to grow tea in India. In 1834 it was officially recognized that in fact indigenous tea trees grew wild, unrecognized, in the hills of Assam. A fierce debate raged as to whether these were identical with the Chinese variety, and whether *Thea* was a separate genus or part of the genus *Camellia*. It was finally settled by the International Code of Botanical Nomenclature in 1905 that the tea tree's correct name, no matter where it grows, is *Camellia sinensis (L.) O. Kuntze*.

The tea tree is in fact native to the whole monsoon area of southeast Asia: Thailand, Burma, southwest China, Assam. There are small variations in the tea trees growing in different plantations and regions, but the differences between them are not sufficient to justify giving them different names. They are known as "cultivars."

A Universal Way of Tea

If the wisdom of the Venerable Hyodang and the teachings of other Korean tea masters are to spread beyond the limits of a small group of people inside Korea, it will have to be in a far more essential and universal form. To cultivate the specific Way of Tea he taught, it is not necessary, we might say, to drink the kind of tea he drank or to have studied the texts about tea that he studied. It is not necessary to be deeply versed in an Asian culture, or in an Asian religious tradition. Otherwise his intuition that "Tea has no Doors" would not be true.

He had the conviction that to drink tea was something far more significant than gulping down a beverage to quench thirst or revive energy. In his own Buddhist tradition, he could express that as the "Seon of Tea" and in today's world, a lot of people are attracted by Buddhism and by the notion of Seon, often without much awareness of what is implied. Perhaps we might need to affirm that even that is not important. Some are attracted by the exoticism of ancient religious cultures; many are not.

The modern world is experienced in many ways. It can seem terrifying, violent, exploitative, dominated by forces that oppress and alienate. Contemporary popular culture is certainly not much interested in refinement or depth of sensibility. We who drink tea sense that inwardness needs to be reasserted, that individual freedom must be conquered, it is not something that can be bought with a credit card on the Internet. It is in this context that the Panyaro Way of Tea, the Seon of Tea if you like, can find its most universal value.

When the Panyaro Way of Hyodang states that "the best is drinking tea alone," it is not being antisocial or elitist. It is saying that no one can attain a properly autonomous level of existence if they never take the time to stop and simply "be" what they most truly are. "Well-being" is the modern term, or "quality of life," but often that only expresses a dissatisfaction, and often advocates a commercial solution. As exemplified by the Panyaro Way of Tea, it encapsulates a practical Way which can lead surprisingly far by its very simplicity.

As already said, it is not necessary to have a box of very rare Panyaro Tea, to know all the oriental tea classics, or even to imitate each of the actions of a Korean tea ceremony. It is certainly not necessary to speak or look Korean. The great intuition of the Venerable Hyodang was to see that the gestures of a very simple, fundamental human activity, the act of preparing and drinking tea, could be quite easily mastered, so that it no longer needs thought but instead allows the practitioner a space in which simply to be and to come to a clearer awareness of what "being" involves.

Buddhists practice Seon and other forms of meditation, Hindu and Taoist traditions have their forms of Yoga, Christians practice contemplative meditation. There is a thirst for such a dimension in many who today know nothing of any religious traditions and wish for none. The Way of Tea can be significant for any and for all. It is not important to ask where it can lead. Certainly no one would embark on such a Way with intense spiritual ambitions, for it does not offer lofty feats of asceticism, or strange states of heightened awareness. That is one of the signs of its authenticity. It is a poor, simple Way, not really needing a capital "W" to justify itself. Take the time, it says, no matter who you are or where in the world you are. Take the time to stop. Be alone with yourself or a few others in a world where a lot of people are alone in the crowd; be quiet in a world where a lot of people are afraid of silence, always listening to music or shouting into a phone. Stopping, alone, in a simple space with just the minimum needed to make tea and drink it. That is the essential practice of the Way of Tea. It is a far remove from the complicated, self-conscious complexities of a formal Tea Ceremony.

There is more to be said, of course. Tea is a wonderful thing in itself; that a single plant's leaves are capable of producing such a

variety of tastes in the hands of expert tea-makers is nothing short of a miracle. Science says that many precious substances are made available to the body in a cup of tea. There is a variety of possible initial responses, either aesthetic or dietetic. Some drink tea for their physical health, others for the refinement of taste, the almost gastronomic delight it can provide. But those must remain secondary aspects. After all, the total experience is more complex, and more ironic, for as we savor the sometimes extraordinarily rich taste of the first cup of well-made tea, we have begun a process involving diminution and loss. The level of tea drops with each sip until the cup is empty; the second and third cups offer a decreasingly intense taste. By the end the leaves have yielded their treasure and lie in the pot exhausted, the ceremony closes. There is an ending. The door must open, the return to activity outside is an obligation.

It is only when the entire process is lived as a unity of experience, valuable and meaningful in itself, that it can become a spiritual way. The aesthete wants to stay at the beginning, with the pleasure. The health-fiend is only thinking of the future benefits, not the event itself. The Way of Tea invites us to a recognition of the fragility, the transient nature of all experience, the value of very simple things, the wonderful treasures made available to us in a tea-leaf thanks to human skills. But above all it offers a moment in which to savor that precise moment, instead of running all the time out of the past towards the future without any way of being

present to the presents offered by the present. The Way of Tea offers presence of mind and mindfulness in a mindless, abstracted world. It is to be hoped that it can spread far and wide, truly universal as it is, as one little but precious element in the endless struggle to assert the value of the truly human against the forces that would deprive us of our essential being. In that way it can truly become one precious part of the Way of Peace we all long to

Congratulatory Message

B orn in England, Brother Anthony arrived in Korea in 1980, invited by Cardinal Kim Sou-Hwan. For more than twenty-five years he has lived his religious vocation here, teaching and visiting every corner of our country. He has developed a deep understanding of our traditional culture, with a particular affection for Korea's traditional tea culture.

I have known him for more than ten years now. In the course of my more than forty years of tea practice, I attach a particular significance to my encounter with him. He has produced beautiful translations of the Seon (Zen)-Tea lectures I give in my little Panyaro Institute for the Way of Tea in Seoul's Insa-dong neighborhood, so that I can distribute them when I am invited abroad to present the Korean Way of Tea. He has also made them available to a worldwide audience through the Internet. These include a history of Korean tea, an exposition of the link between Seon and tea, and an explanation of the particular method used to make my Panyaro tea.

Often, in the tea-making season in May, Brother Anthony has traveled down to the remote rural valley where I make Panyaro tea, together with students and friends, to savor the freshly made tea and enjoy its unique fragrance. It is almost as though he was Korean in a previous existence, so deep and spontaneous is his love of Korean food, tea, and traditional Korean houses.

It is a source of great satisfaction that Brother Anthony has at last written a text expressing his deep knowledge of Korean tea and combined that with beautiful photographs to produce a guidebook destined for an international readership. Moreover, helping him in this task is one of the graduates of my Panyaro Institute, Hwachon Hong Kyeong-Hee, who has contributed his knowledge of tea poetry and the methods by which tea is made. He has long been serving as Brother Anthony's guide to Korean culture and it was he who first introduced him to me.

I feel sure that this volume, produced by two such highly qualified practitioners of the Way of Tea, will make it possible for people from many countries to easily understand and appreciate this vital but little-known aspect of Korea's culture.

Won-Hwa Chae Jeong-bok
Director of the Panyaro Institute for the Way of Tea, in Seoul.

Epilogue for 2022

This little book was first published in 2007 and has been reprinted five times. Many tea friends around the world have expressed their affection for it and that is surely mainly thanks to the photos and beautiful layout provided by the design team at Seoul Selection. It has been used in several places across the world as a textbook for classes introducing students and others to the Way of Tea, and that is very satisfying. Asked late in 2021 whether there is anything that needs to be changed for a sixth reprint, we see one lack which needs to be remedied. When the book was written, Korean tea was almost exclusively green tea, and we described in detail the process by which green tea is dried and served. At that time, the oxidized (or "fermented") form of Korean tea was virtually unknown, to most tea-drinkers at least. Over the last fifteen years, that has changed and the tea usually known as Balhyocha (or "yellow tea," or "fermented tea,") has become the most popular form, probably because its taste is far sweeter and "nuttier" than the often insipid or tart taste of green tea. Balhyocha is produced by many makers following various slightly different processes and the result is usually close to a delicate red or black tea, rather than the oolong teas of China to which it is sometimes compared.

Since we are mainly going to reprint the book as it has always existed, this Epilogue seems the best place to describe very simply the basic process by which Balhyocha is made. The tea is picked as for green tea, in late April then through to the end of May, plucking the tender new shoots and avoiding stems as much as possible. For Balhyocha, the picked leaves are not dried quickly but are allowed to wilt for several hours, often overnight, spread on shallow bamboo trays. This wilting is also a basic process for Chinese oolong teas, changing and intensifying the fragrance. The most important feature of Balhyocha is that the process does not involve roasting. Instead, several kilograms of the wilted leaves are piled on a table covered with a cloth or straw mat, to be rolled cold. A number of people share out handfuls of the leaves and roll them gently but vigorously on the surface of the table, softening them and exposing the juices in the leaves to the air without breaking the leaves. Each person rolls a clutch of leaves for several minutes, then passes that to the person beside them, and so round the table. This continues until the leaves are thoroughly rolled, the juices exposed to the oxidizing effect of the air.

Then all the juicy batches of tea are collected together and placed in a pottery hangari (an onggi pot). This is placed in a room in which the floor has been heated to forty or even fifty degrees Celsius, wrapped in a blanket, for several hours. Ideally this accelerates the oxidizing process without involving the enzymes suggested by the word "fermented," although this is not always certain. Then the leaves are removed from the pot and spread on sheets of paper laid on the hot floor. There they slowly dry, for several days. Some makers accelerate the drying by using a heated cauldron as for green tea but the slower process probably helps to intensify the flavor. The tea is then allowed to rest and breathe for some time before being packed. It is brewed in the same manner as green tea, but the water should be hot, not far from boiling. As for green tea, the brewing time should be quite short, and then the tea should be completely poured off the leaves. Usually Balhyocha can be brewed more often than green tea, not losing its taste for six or more brews.

One other form of tea that was not covered in our original text is the "caked tea" which the great scholar Dasan Jeong Yak-yong developed during his exile in Gangjin (South Jeolla Province) at the start of the 19th century, following the instructions he found in Lu Yu's "Tea Classic," and which the Ven. Choui then made popular among his high-class acquaintances in Seoul. This is usually called "ttokcha" (cake-tea) or "Doncha / Yeopjeoncha / Dongjeoncha / Dancha" (cash-tea) because it is made by steaming fresh tea leaves and pounding them to a mush, which is than shaped into small rounds like rice cakes or old coins, pierced in the center, and strung on a string or stick to dry slowly. Naturally, this means that the leaves will oxidize by prolonged exposure to the air. Sometimes they may become slightly mildewed. Hung in a well-ventilated space, they have to dry and oxidize for several months before being packed. Or they may remain hanging until the time comes to brew some. The (usually quite small) cakes are roasted over a smokeless charcoal brazier to remove any mold and bring out the taste. They are then boiled for up to an hour, since they are much slower to release their taste, color and fragrance than other kinds of tea. This caked tea is still uncommon and usually hard to find.

Korea produces very little tea, only about 3,000 tons in a year, much of which is not tea for drinking but for confectionary or cosmetics. Only a very small amount is exported for sale outside of Korea, mostly the highest quality hand-processed tea, produced by individual masters. Inside of Korea it is very rare to find tea-rooms serving and selling good Korean tea, except in Seoul's Insadong and at quite a few temples. Instead, Taiwanese "bubble tea" franchises have sprung up, while Starbucks also offers their version of Korean green tea. Korea has a great number of coffee shops run by coffee experts, but tea remains unknown among the younger generation. No attractive form of modern marketing seems to have been found. We can only hope that this book might help people discover the beauty and fragrance of Korea's tea before the tea fields are all replaced by coffee plantations! With our best wishes for happy tea!

About the Authors

Brother Anthony of Taizé was born in 1942 in England. He is a member of the Community of Taizé. Since 1980, he has been living in Korea, where he taught for many years at Sogang University. He has published some 60 volumes of English translations of modern Korean literature, mostly poetry but also some popular novels. He and Hong Kyeong-hee also published 'Korean Tea Classics,' a collection of 3 fundamental texts about tea from the Joseon era.

Hong Kyeong-hee was born in North
Jeolla Province in 1957 and was first
introduced to the practice of green tea
during a stay at Geumsan-sa temple (near
Gimje) in 1974. He studied the Hyodang
tradition of the Zen of Tea and now
practices tea in that tradition, producing
his own tea in a wild tea field near
Hwaeomsa temple in Gurye, South Jeolla
Province. He has given presentations of the
Korean tea ceremony in a number of
countries, including the UK and the USA.